The mountains are calling and I must go.
– John Muir

THE COLLECTIBLE PHOTO GUIDE

COLORADO SPRINGS

Book design and photography by Jeff Lammers & Connie Chapin
Text by Connie Chapin
Design contribution and photography by Leah Shockley
Graphics and layout by Sarah Ballard

A special thank you to Visit Colorado Springs for their generous assistance with photos and information. **VisitCOS.com** is a valuable place to learn more about this exciting area and all it has to offer.

Although the Broadmoor Hotel and Seven Falls are a significant part of Colorado Springs, they declined to be featured in our book.

Dedicated to our "Deerest" friend, Rosie

Photo Credits:
p 10 Will Rogers Shrine - Frank Winkelmann, p 13 Cheyenne Mtn Park Sign - Jeffrey Beall, p 14 Lightbulb - Manitou Springs Creative District, p 15 Fine Arts Center – JAKeeran, p 16 Cog train in station - Milan Suvajac, p 30-31 - The Antlers and The Mining Exchange Hotel, p 32-33 - Cheyenne Mountain Zoo, p 39 - Sculpture - David Shankbone, p 44-45 Arcade, Fountain, Creek – Manitou Springs, p 48-49 Cave of the Winds, p 52 - Falls – Ahodges7, p 55 Penrose Heritage Museum, p 57 Coins - Money Museum, p59 May Museum, p 61 Motorcycle Museum, p 62 Castle – Jeffrey Beall, p 63 Fine Arts Center, p 64-65 The North Pole, p 66-67 - Space Foundation, p 68–69 Dinosaur Resource Center, p 70-71 The Mining Museum , p 72 Runner - Matt Carpenter, p 76 - Motorcycle - Hustvedt, Peugeot - Jake Archibald, road - SS, White car - Chris Rojas, p 81 Train - Drew Jacksich, p 92 - Dredge, Creek - goodfreephotos.com, p 96-97 Florissant Fossil Beds, p 106 - Fish – JSMclaren,

Books available in quantity for corporate use or incentives.
For ordering information please visit us on **TravelKeepsakes.com**

ISBN: 978-1-7328419-0-1

Printed in the United States of America
First Printing January 2019
10 9 8 7 6 5 4 3 2 1

Table of Contents

Table of Contents *(Continued)*

Family Fun

Annual events

Nearby

The Great Outdoors

An Impressive Trail *of* History....

Native tribes were the first people to make what we now call the "Pikes Peak Region" their home. In about 500 A.D., Ute people arrived in the region. Impressed by the majestic mountain, they named it *Ta-Wa-Ah-Gath,* which means Sun Mountain, for the way its slopes reflect the sun's rays.

A band of that Ute tribe called Tabeguache, which means People of Sun Mountain, settled here. During a period of about two hundred years, before the arrival of the white settler, Comanche, Kiowa, Cheyenne, Arapahoe and Sioux also occupied the region ... Pawnee and Apache frequently visited and hunted here. The Arapahoe people knew the mountains as *Heey-otoyoo,* meaning Long Mountain. Early Spanish explorers named the mountain *El Capitan* ("The Leader").

When Anglo-American explorer Zebulon Pike arrived in the region in November 1806, he and a small group of men set out to climb *Grand Peak* (that's what they called the mountain). After a failed attempt to climb to the top, Pike wrote in his journal:

...here we found the snow middle deep; no sign of beast or bird inhabiting this region. The thermometer which stood at 9° above 0 at the foot of the mountain, here fell to 4° below 0. The summit of the Grand Peak, which was entirely bare of vegetation and covered with snow, now appeared at the distance of 15 or 16 miles from us, and as high again as what we had ascended, and would have taken a whole day's march to have arrived at its base, when I believed no human being could have ascended to its pinnacle. This with the condition of my soldiers who had only light overalls on, and no stockings, and every way ill provided to endure the inclemency of the region; the bad prospect of killing any thing to subsist on, with the further detention of two or three days, which it must occasion, determined us to return.

[Pike, Zebulon M. (1810) "An Account of Expeditions to the Sources of the Mississippi"]

Zebulon Pike
1779-1813

It took another 14 years for Pikes Peak to be conquered! The first explorer to reach the summit was naturalist Dr. Edwin James in the summer of 1820.

Even though Pike's expedition never made it to the top, still, in 1840, the mountain was officially named Pike's Peak. In 1890, the United States Board of Geographic Names simplified the name to "Pikes Peak".

In the foothills of Pikes Peak, the town of Colorado City was founded during the region's gold rush in 1859. Colorado City was the first capital of the Colorado Territory and the main supply camp for the area's mining industry. Residents of Colorado City worked at some of the region's 50 coalmines. The town was known for its saloons, brothels, gambling rooms and even opium dens. Tunnels under Colorado Avenue ensured that men could enter these businesses without being seen.

General William Jackson Palmer

El Paso County was formed in 1861 and Colorado City was the county seat until 1873, when the courthouse moved to Colorado Springs.

In 1869, General William Jackson Palmer, a Civil War hero from Pennsylvania, visited the region for the first time and fell in love with its "most enticing scenery." He returned in 1870 with a grand vision for a sophisticated town, befitting his cultured wife, Queen.

In 1871, Palmer's vision became reality with the founding of Colorado Springs. A year later, he founded the town of Manitou (now Manitou Springs). This quaint little town at the base of Pikes Peak had its beginning as a resort area nicknamed "Little London" because of its popularity with English tourists.

William and Queen Palmer resided in Glen Eyrie, a 22-room castle, the General had built for his beloved wife. Queen opened the first public school in Colorado Springs in November of 1871, while her husband founded the Denver and Rio Grande Railroad. His vision was to bring people suffering from poor health, especially tuberculosis, from the East Coast to the dry, sunny and mild climate of Colorado Springs.

Glen Eyrie Castle

In 1883, Palmer built the Antler Hotel, one of Colorado Springs' major landmarks.

Original Antlers hotel
1883-1898 – burned down

He also opened the Colorado College, funded libraries, a tuberculosis sanatorium, the Colorado School for the Deaf and Blind, and founded the Colorado Springs Gazette.

"Could one live in constant view of these grand mountains without being elevated by them into a lofty plane of thought and purpose?"

– General William Jackson Palmer

In the 1890s, gold was discovered on the western slope of Pikes Peak! It was one of the richest gold strikes in American history. The Cripple Creek Mining District grew almost overnight to be home to more than 50,000 people! By the turn of the 19th century, nearby Colorado Springs was labeled "The City of Millionaires." One of these millionaires was Spencer Penrose. He, too, had made his first fortune in Cripple Creek and used his vast resources to build the Pikes Peak and Cheyenne Mountain Highways. He also established the Cheyenne Mountain Zoo, Will Rogers Shrine and The Broadmoor Hotel.

Spencer Penrose

Broadmoor • Circa 1918

Cripple Creek • Circa 1900

Katherine Lee Bates

In the summer of 1893, Katharine Lee Bates, a professor of English literature at Wellesley College in Massachusetts, visited Colorado Springs to teach a short summer school session at Colorado College. One day, during her stay, along with other teachers, Katharine Lee Bates made a trip to the top of Pikes Peak. There, describing the extraordinary view, she said, "It was then and there, as I was looking out over the sea-like expanse of fertile country spreading away so far under those ample skies, that the opening lines of the hymn floated into my mind". On July 4, 1895, "America the Beautiful" appeared for the first time in print. A few months later, the lyrics were set to music by Silas G. Pratt.

From Small Beginnings...

Intrigued by the region's captivating beauty, the sunny climate and countless attractions, the stream of tourists has never subsided since its beginnings in 1871. Instead, with more than 20 million tourists annually, tourism is now the third largest industry in the area.

Today's Colorado Springs is the second largest city in Colorado. It sits at an impressive 6,035 feet above sea level and boasts an average of 243 days of sunshine per year. Its location, just east of the Rocky Mountains, subjects Colorado Springs at times to drastically changing weather conditions; thunderstorms with multitudes of severe lightning strikes and golf ball size hail are not uncommon.

Will Rogers Shrine of the Sun

Denver & Rio Grande Railroad Depot

DOUGH ROOM

Colorado Springs is home to the United States Olympic Committee and Training Center and many Olympic coaches and athletes. It is also known for its strong military presence ... five military bases are located in the region, including the renowned United States Air Force Academy.

US Olympic Training Center

Fort Carson

Located on Cheyenne Mountain, *The Cheyenne Mountain Complex* is home to the Cheyenne Mountain Air Force Station. This underground facility was built for the North American Aerospace Defense Command (NORAD). The United States and Canada created NORAD in 1957. The purpose for this bi-national organization was to create a centralized control center for air defenses against the threat of Soviet bombers and missiles. After the end of the Cold War and a major renovation, the location now conducts aerospace and maritime warning and control in the defense of North America. There is no public access to the facility.

Arts and Culture

The beauty of Colorado Springs has inspired artists from around the country. Many filmmakers, visual artists, writers and musicians have made the Pikes Peak region their home. With more than 400 local arts and cultural groups here, you can attend a live music performance, see a play, visit a gallery or enjoy fine dining on any given night.

KNOW BEFORE YOU GO

Download the free app **"Otocast"** for a self-guided audio tour through downtown Colorado Springs.

Greetings from a Historic Landmark

When Zalmon Simmons, the founder of the Simmons Beautyrest Mattress Company, reached the summit of Pikes Peak in the late 1880s, although exhausted from the grueling two-day trip on a mule, he was so mesmerized by the scenery that he decided the views should be experienced by many ... but in a more comfortable manner. Hence, in 1891, the Pikes Peak Cog Railway was established! It was the highest cog railway train in North America, climbing to the almost insurmountable 14,115 feet summit of Pikes Peak Mountain.

A "Cog Train" uses a set of steel teeth in the middle of the track to pull itself up steep grades.

After more than a century of climbing up and down the 8.9-mile track, due to maintenance issues, the railway was shut down after the 2017 season.

It is predicted that the railway could remain closed for up to three years, but there is promise that it will reopen once again with a new and improved design, built to last another century.

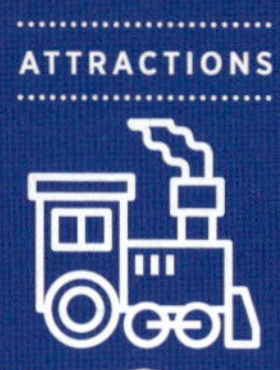

Pikes Peak

Globally the second most visited mountain, Pikes Peak stands at a whopping 14,115 feet above sea level and is one of the only 14ers in the world that's accessible by car.

The 19 mile long paved Pikes Peak Highway takes you to the top of the mountain; exhilarating hairpin switchbacks and roadside pull-off stations with the most breathtaking views make this an exciting drive.

FUN FACT!

On the clearest days, **you can see five states** (Colorado, Arizona, New Mexico, Utah and Kansas)

SUMMIT
PIKES PEAK 14,115ft
PIKE National Forest

But the views aren't the only things that make this majestic drive unforgettable! There is an abundance of wildlife for you to discover. Look out for Rocky Mountain Bighorn sheep, marmots, mountain lions, bears and more!

Garden of the Gods Park

Garden OF THE Gods

Welcome to your one-stop paradise! Imagine dramatic views of unique 300 ft. towering sandstone rock formations against a backdrop of snow-capped Pikes Peak and bright blue skies...

GARDEN OF THE GODS
VISITOR & NATURE CENTER
COLORADO SPRINGS

Stop by the world-class Visitor & Nature Center and explore this amazing 1300-acre park in an all-new fun and interactive way: experience the new Geo-Trekker Theater and learn how these amazing red rocks got here. Take in the majestic views from inside the glass-enclosed café or from the expansive terrace.

Or just sit and simply let your soul enjoy the breathtaking views of Pikes Peak and Garden of the Gods.

Kissing Camels
Balanced Rock

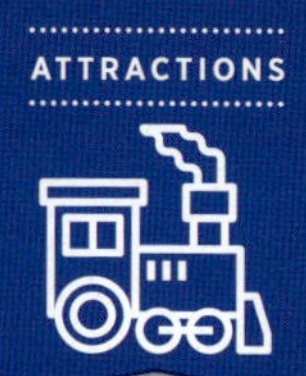

The Antlers Hotel

When General William Jackson Palmer founded Colorado Springs in 1871, he dreamed of creating a first class hotel. His dream came to life in June of 1883 when The Antlers hotel opened its doors! Sadly the hotel burned to the ground in 1898 only to be rebuilt in 1901. The new Antlers hotel flourished until 1964, when it was torn down. It was replaced with the fabulous hotel you see today!

Today The Antlers, A Wyndham Hotel, hosts many conventions. Travelers from around the world get to enjoy a multitude of restaurants and a 24-hour state of the art health club. Since the hotel is located in the heart of Colorado Springs, museums, art galleries, boutiques and restaurants are all a quick walk away.

The Antlers – June 1883

The Antlers – 1901 to 1964

The Mining Exchange Hotel

The Mining Exchange, a Wyndham Grand Hotel & Spa, is an exquisite boutique hotel in downtown Colorado Springs. Just like it's sister hotel, The Antlers, The Mining Exchange has an impressive history to look back on. Built in the early 1900s to house the Colorado Springs Mining Exchange it quickly became known as "the handsomest, the largest and most substantial structure in the city".

In 2012, after having sat vacant for many years, extensive renovations brought this beautiful Italian Renaissance style structure back to life. Its original grandeur was restored and a magnificent piece of architecture preserved!

Today, The Mining Exchange greets guests from around the world with its historic charm, modern-day elegance and luxury comforts.

Cheyenne Mountain Zoo

Cheyenne Mountain Zoo, America's only mountain zoo, is home to over 750 animals from 170 different species.

Whether you soar above the zoo on the Mountaineer Sky Ride, enjoy a carousel ride or hand-feed giraffes or birds in the Australian aviary, this zoo offers fun for everyone. Combine this with its picturesque location and breathtaking views of the city and the plains, a visit to Cheyenne Mountain Zoo is guaranteed to make your day memorable!

FUN FACT!

Cheyenne Mountain Zoo has **the largest giraffe herd** of any zoo in the world!

CHEYENNE
MOUNTAIN
ZOO
ELEVATION 6714 FEET

You will have a hard time imagining Old Colorado City's rough past when you stroll down the tree-lined avenues! From galleries, museums, boutiques, charming restaurants and coffee houses to farmers markets, outdoor-concerts and festivals ... this charming town has it all!

Old Colorado City

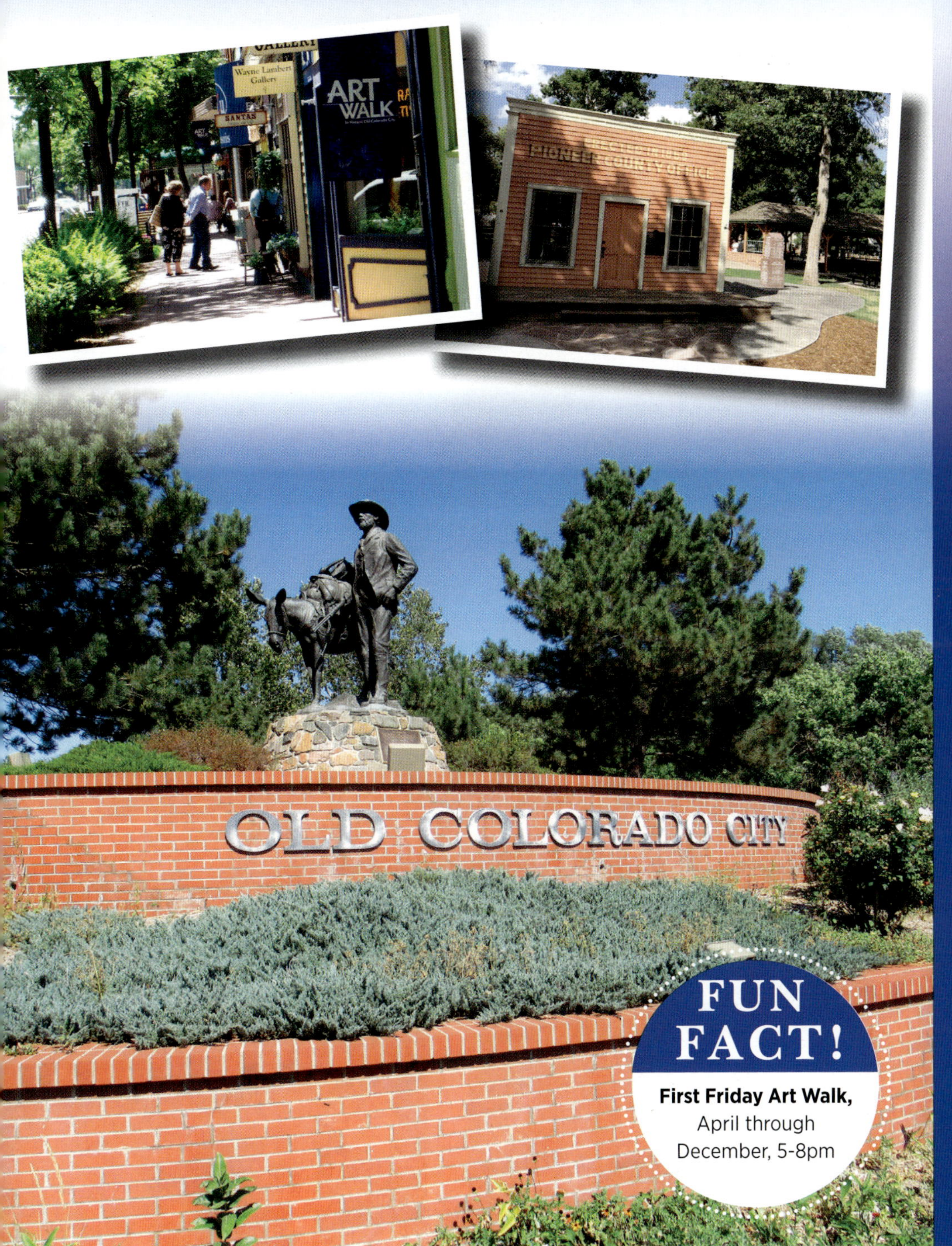

FUN FACT!

First Friday Art Walk, April through December, 5-8pm

Red Rock Canyon Open Space

Just south of US-24, between Colorado Springs and Manitou Springs, Red Rock Canyon Open Space awaits you with an abundance of natural erosive architecture.

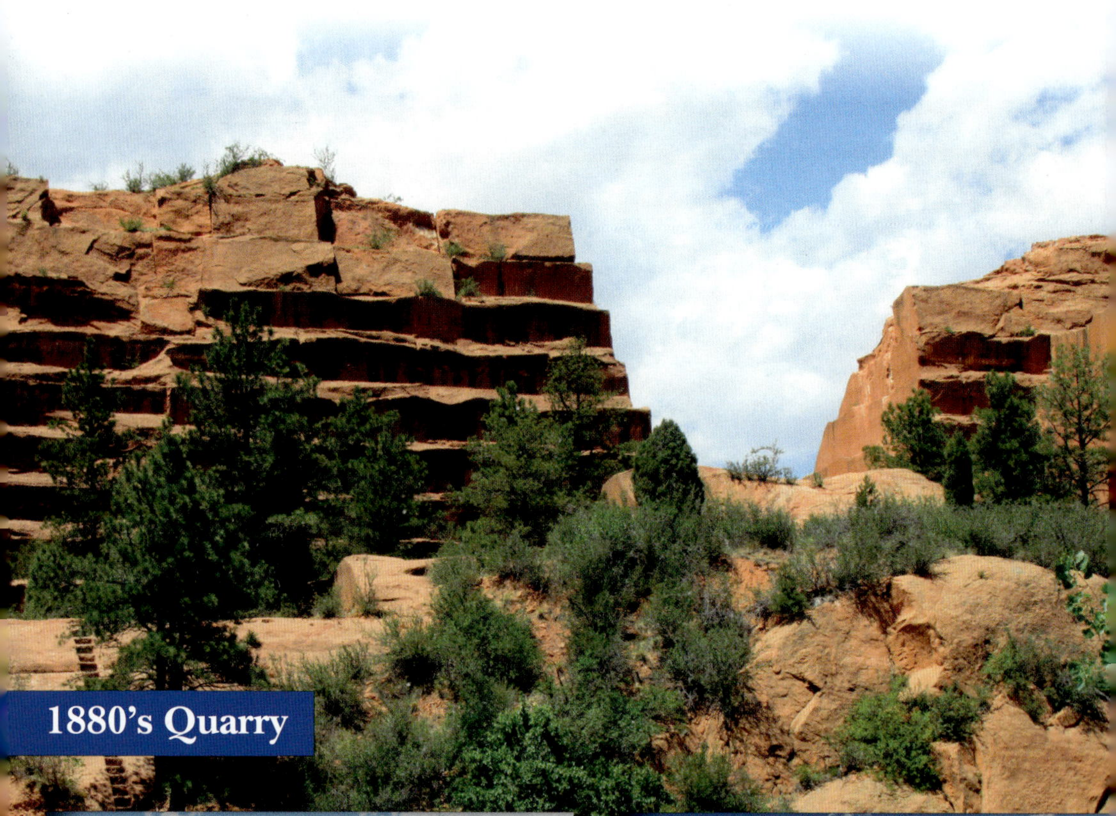

1880's Quarry

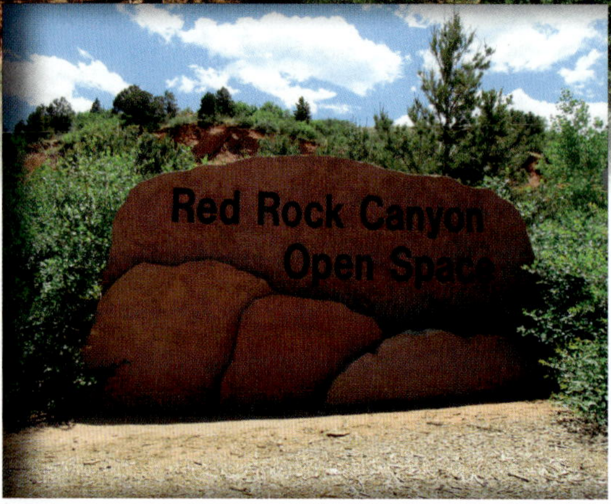

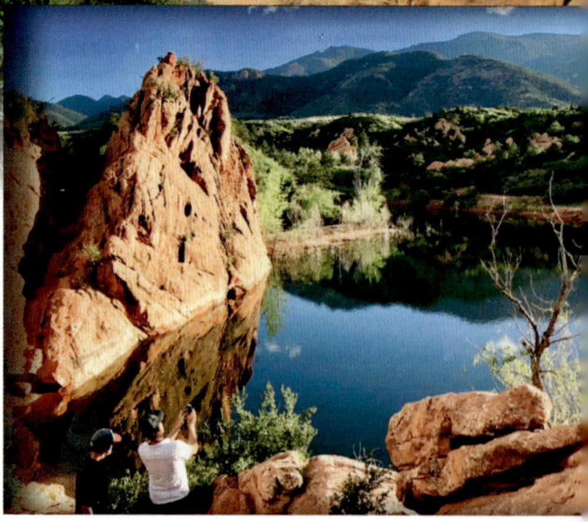

Trails wind through picturesque canyons, over ridges, even stone quarries, and take you around a beautiful lake. There are picnic areas and scenic overlooks, an off-leash dog park and a free-ride bicycle stunt park. Running, hiking, biking, horseback riding, and rock climbing – its all done here!

Something INTERESTING

Here, the **Ute Indians** would stand and watch over the plains.

U.S. Olympic Complex

Colorado Springs, aka Olympic City USA, is home to the US Olympic Committee Headquarters and the US Olympic Training Center. The mild climate and superb natural training grounds along with the city's awe-inspiring beauty draw many aspiring athletes to the region.

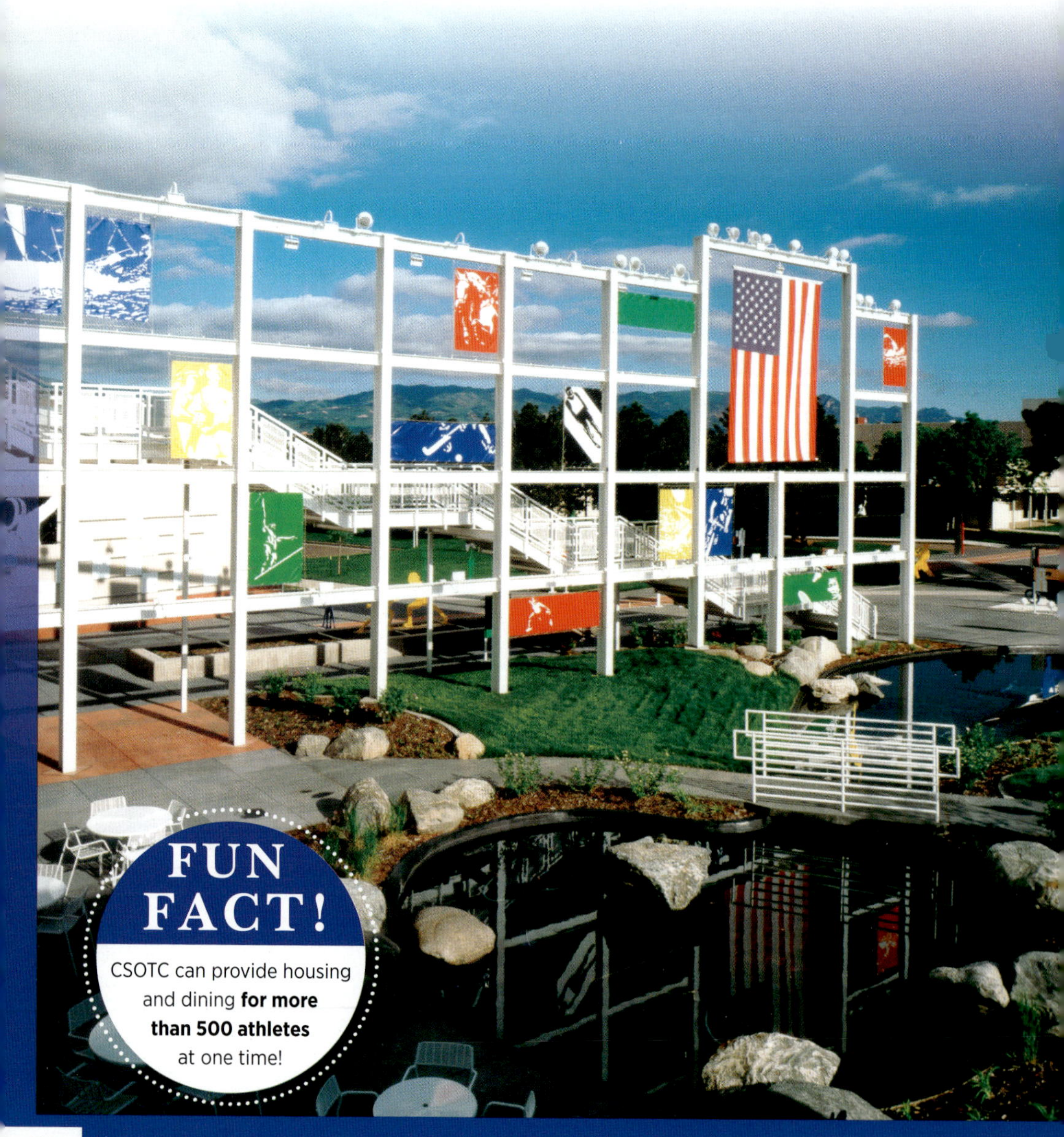

FUN FACT!

CSOTC can provide housing and dining **for more than 500 athletes** at one time!

The training center houses sport facilities for Olympic disciplines like Boxing, Cycling, Figure Skating, Gymnastics, Judo, Pentathlon, Shooting, Swimming and Wrestling.

Various guided tours are available Monday through Saturday.

U.S. Air Force Academy

Founded in 1954, the United States Air Force Academy houses over 4,000 undergraduate students, referred to as cadets, as they go through rigorous military schooling and training.

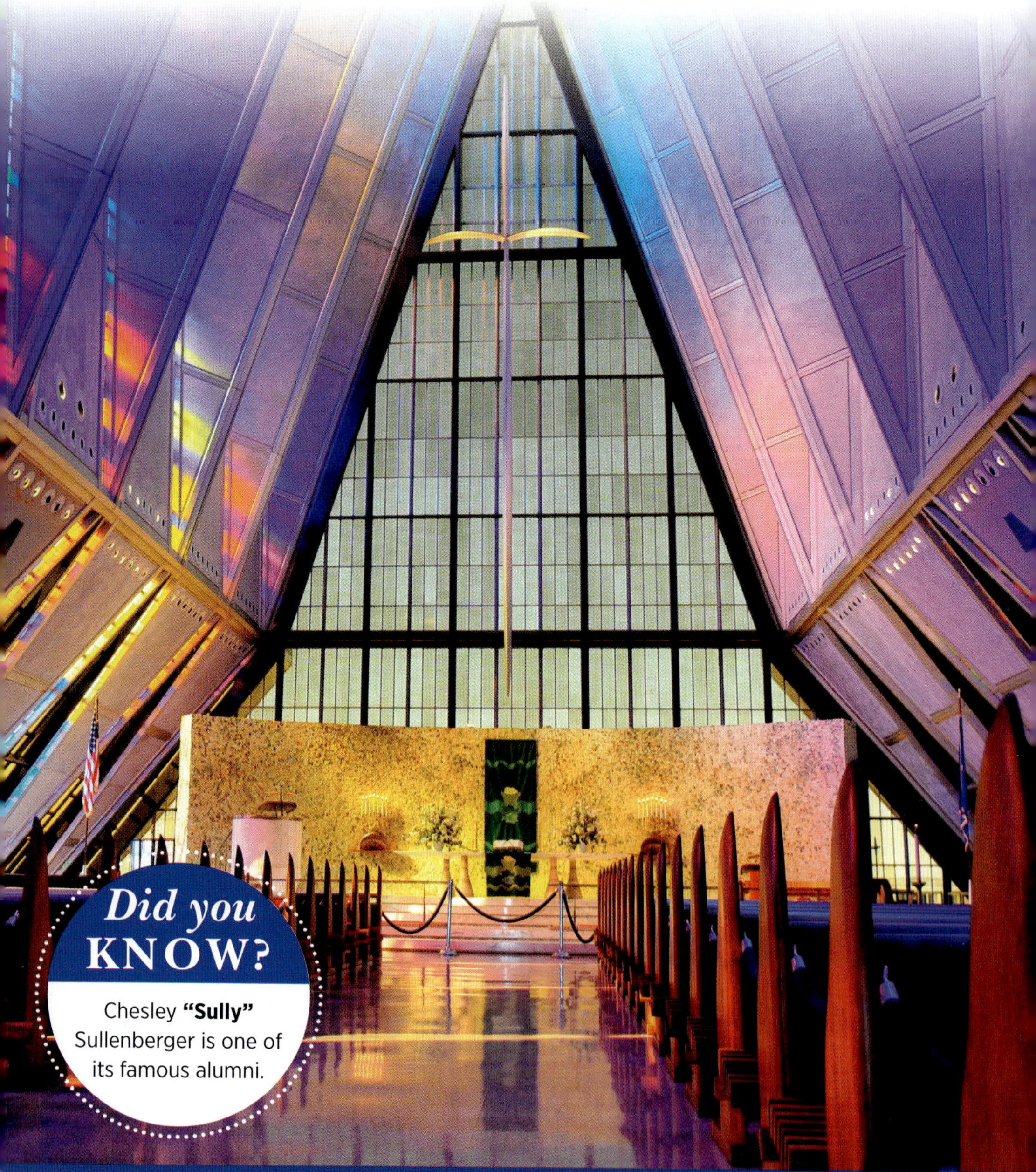

Did you KNOW?

Chesley **"Sully"** Sullenberger is one of its famous alumni.

Although the student body and the grounds are impressive, the true reason to visit this 18,500-acre campus are for both, the stunning views and The Barry Goldwater Visitor Center. Referred to as the gateway to the Air Force Academy, this 31,600-square-foot building features an impressive exhibit, a snack bar and a gift shop. The visitor center has free admission and is open to the public from 9 a.m. to 5 p.m.

ATTRACTIONS
COLORADO SPRINGS
Helen Hunt Falls
Silver Cascade Trail 1/3 mile
Degree of difficulty- moderate to difficult, with slippery gravel, and a 200 ft. rise in elevation
Appropriate shoes recommended
Park Open:
May 1 to Oct 31 • 5am – 11pm
Nov 1 to Apr 30 • 5am – 9pm
Please Observe the Following:
·Dogs Must be on a Leash
·Owner Must Remove Pet's Waste
·No Alcohol Consumption
No Camping
No Littering or Dumping
No Discharging of Firearms
Climbing with a Permit Only

Helen Hunt Falls

Located in beautiful North Cheyenne Cañon Park, scenic Helen Hunt Falls is a "must see". The falls are named in honor of Helen Hunt Jackson, an American poet and activist for Native Americans. Helen loved the area, especially North Cheyenne Cañon Park, so much that she was buried here in 1885.

Admire the views from the base of the falls or take the steps to the bridge above. Up for more? Hike up the Silver Cascade Trail! This moderate 0.7-mile hike with an elevation gain of 200 feet will not disappoint with beautiful views of the canyon and the Front Range.

GOOD *to Know*

Best time to visit: Spring to early summer when the snow is melting.

Manitou Springs

Walk around Manitou Springs and you will know where it got its name ..."Manitou", the Native American word for "great spirit" couldn't be more fitting for this exuberant little town at the base of Pikes Peak that boasts trading posts, art galleries, gift shops, restaurants and eclectic neighborhoods.

Enjoy a sip of the naturally carbonated mineral spring water! Eight fountains are located throughout the historic town of this Rocky Mountain marvel.

FUN FACT!

Manitou Springs was nicknamed **"Little London"**

ATTRACTIONS

Manitou Incline

The Manitou Incline was originally built as a cable car to carry materials to build pipelines on Pikes Peak. Once the work was completed, it quickly transitioned into a tourist attraction until a rockslide washed out the tracks and closed it down. The rails were removed but the railroad ties remained, creating a massive 2,744-step staircase. Famous for it's sweeping views, the Manitou Incline is now one of the most popular and challenging hikes in the area.

FUN FACT!

The trail gains **2,000 feet** in elevation!

Cave of the Winds

Cave of the Winds, located at the base of Pikes Peak in Manitou Springs, is one of America's most spectacular show caves.

Looking for a fun experience for the whole family? Take them on a 45 minute guided tour through a mile of winding caverns. Feeling adventurous? Choose the 1.5-hour Lantern Tour ... Grab a lantern and explore the rugged caverns just like the early explorers did.

Once you resurface, there are plenty of above ground adventures awaiting you and your family.

Reach new heights on the "Wind Walker" challenge course, a ropes course high up in the sky or take a dare devil plunge off a 200 foot cliff on the "Terror-Dactyl", the first-of-its-kind ride in the world. Still want more? The "Bat-A-Pult" takes you high up in the skies in this 1,200-foot high aerial ride. Feel like rock-climbing like a pro? Give the exhilarating guided canyon climbing tour "Via Ferrata Canyon Tours" a try!

C. Weitfle's Stereoscopic Views.

Rainbow Falls

Rainbow Falls near Manitou Springs is more than just a lovely waterfall; it is a place steeped in history. The Tabeguache, or Sun Mountain people, a band of the Ute Indian tribe, recognized this beautiful spot as a special place after spotting a rainbow in the waterfall's mist. Today, a 0.15-mile trail winds from the parking lot along the picturesque Fountain Creek up to the waterfall. If you're lucky and the timing is right, you may see a rainbow!

FUN FACT!

Nicknamed **Graffiti Falls** thanks to the ever-present art.

ATTRACTIONS
FUN FACT!
A Native American family lived on the premises until **1984.**
MANITOU
CLIFF DWELLINGS
and MUSEUM
NEXT RIGHT →

Manitou Cliff Dwellings

Located in Manitou Springs, at the foot of Pikes Peak, the Manitou Cliff Dwellings are a true historical treasure. In an effort to preserve the fine stonework architecture of the Southwestern Pueblo Indians, these cliff dwellings were relocated from their original site near Mesa Verde between 1904 and 1907. Protected by a red sandstone overhang, these 800 year old Anasazi cliff dwellings promise to amaze and educate.

National Museum of WWII Aviation

A place for the history buff and lover of aviation … the National Museum of World War II Aviation is not to be missed. With more than a dozen flying World War II aircraft on display and many more in the restoration hanger, this museum is certain to bring to life the amazing role aviation played in the “greatest” of all wars.

Penrose Heritage Museum

The Penrose Heritage Museum showcases the history and heritage of the Pikes Peak region through the personal artifact collection of Colorado Springs philanthropists Spencer and Julie Penrose. The museum's exhibits feature an impressive collection of carriages, western cultural artifacts, and a specific tribute to the Pikes Peak International Hill Climb, the second oldest motorsport event in the U.S., started by Spencer Penrose in 1916.

GOOD *to Know*

Free to the public

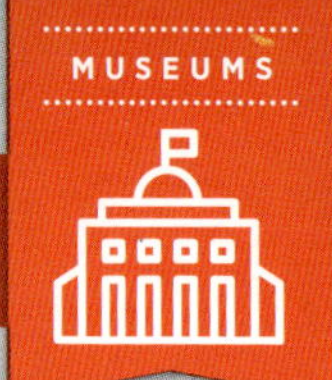

Pioneers Museum

Located in downtown Colorado Springs, in the beautifully restored 1903 El Paso County Courthouse, the Colorado Springs Pioneers Museum (CSPM) gracefully portrays the Pikes Peak region's unique history and culture. CSPM exhibits fascinating topics which include the region's American Indian cultures; western exploration; early settlers who built homes, businesses and communities at the foot of Pikes Peak; and health seekers who came west seeking a cure in this community's clean, dry air. New and innovative exhibits are continually added to engage visitors. Public programs range from scholarly presentations, family festivals, community events, and school field trips. Through all of this, the museum exhibits a remarkable collection of items that emphasize the unique character of this front-range community.

GOOD *to Know*

Free admission, closed Sunday & Monday

GOOD *to Know*

Admission is free for everyone the 3rd Saturday of every month!

Money Museum

The Edward C. Rochette Money Museum is America's largest numismatics museum. The museum explores history, art and science and exhibits spectacular rare coins, including examples from ancient times and the most complete collection of U.S. gold coins.

There is also a Kids Zone and a Mini-Mint, where visitors can see how coins were made from the early 1500s to 1800s. Guided tours of the museum are also available (by reservation only).

On Display:
1913 Liberty Nickel
Valued at $3 million

On Display:
1804 Liberty Dollar
Valued at $4 million

MUSEUMS

KNOW BEFORE YOU GO

Gold panning is seasonal **(May-September)**

Wild West Ghost Town Museum

"Pikes Peak or Bust" ... was the cry that opened the Colorado territory to the gold miners in 1858. After the gold rush was over, many towns were abandoned and became, well, ghost towns.

In 1954, the Ghost Town Museum was created to preserve a piece of that notorious Wild West era. Housed inside a historic 1899 stone structure, the museum greets you with a real late-1800s town! Explore what pioneer life used to be like ... stroll down the historic wooden walking path along historic buildings, horse carriages and artifacts. Visit a saloon or an old-time barbershop. Crank a butter churn, operate an old-time arcade or nickelodeon, or pan for real gold in the panning areas!

May Natural History Museum

Known as the "Bug Museum" to locals, the May Natural History Museum is the place for everyone who is interested in all things creepy and crawly!

Museum founder, James May, traveled the world and brought home over 7,000 different species of beautiful butterflies, moths, giant spiders and deadly scorpions and more than 100,000 exotic specimens of bugs and insects, creating the world's largest private bug collections. Go check it out ... you'll go bug-eyed over this place!

Lester L. Williams Fire Museum

This unique museum is home to the remnants of the original Colorado Springs fire station that was built in 1909. The station closed in 1972 and became part of the Lester L. Williams Fire Museum in 2001. The museum exhibits an impressive collection of fire memorabilia including horse-drawn and motorized pumpers and even a historic 1834 hose wagon. Free admission.

Rocky Mountain Motorcycle Museum

Born to be wild or not ... this museum will spark anyone's interest. It features over 75 fully restored vintage motorcycles from every make and model, some as old as 1913.

The Rocky Mountain Motorcycle Museum opened in 1992 and rests on the values that it would always be free and open to the public.

This is a wonderful way to spend a few hours reflecting on the heritage of these two-wheeled machines.

GOOD *to Know*

Free admission but donations are greatly appreciated.

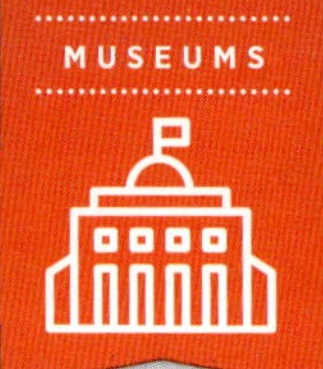

Miramont Castle

Built in the late 1890s by Jean Baptiste Francolon, a French Catholic priest, Miramont Castle will take you back in time to the Victorian era. Take a self-guided tour through 30 stunning castle rooms, beautifully appointed with authentic Victorian furnishings or enjoy a 1890s inspired High Tea in the Queen's Parlour Tearoom, where you can delight in not only the cuisine, but also the spectacular mountain views.

KNOW BEFORE YOU GO

High Tea or Light Victorian Tea **require advance reservations.**

FUN FACT!

Don't miss ...
First Friday Art Parties in the Deco Lounge.

Fine Arts Center and Museum

The Colorado Springs Fine Arts Center at Colorado College is one of the rare multi-discipline arts institutions in the country, bringing together a museum, theater and art school - all under one roof! This crossover of the different art forms results in exciting performances, concerts and amazing exhibits – a benefit for everyone!

FAMILY FUN

North Pole
Home of Santa's Workshop

Christmas in July? Or May? Even October? Yes, it's Christmas all year!! Here the Christmas spirit lasts year round.

Christmas music fills the air while you browse this cozy village. With an arcade, magic shows and more than 25 rides, this Christmas themed amusement park offers fun for the whole family.

Space Foundation Discovery Center

The Space Foundation Discovery Center is the region's only dedicated space, science and technology center and museum. Visitors learn through interactive activities about space exploration by utilizing science, technology, engineering, art and mathematics.

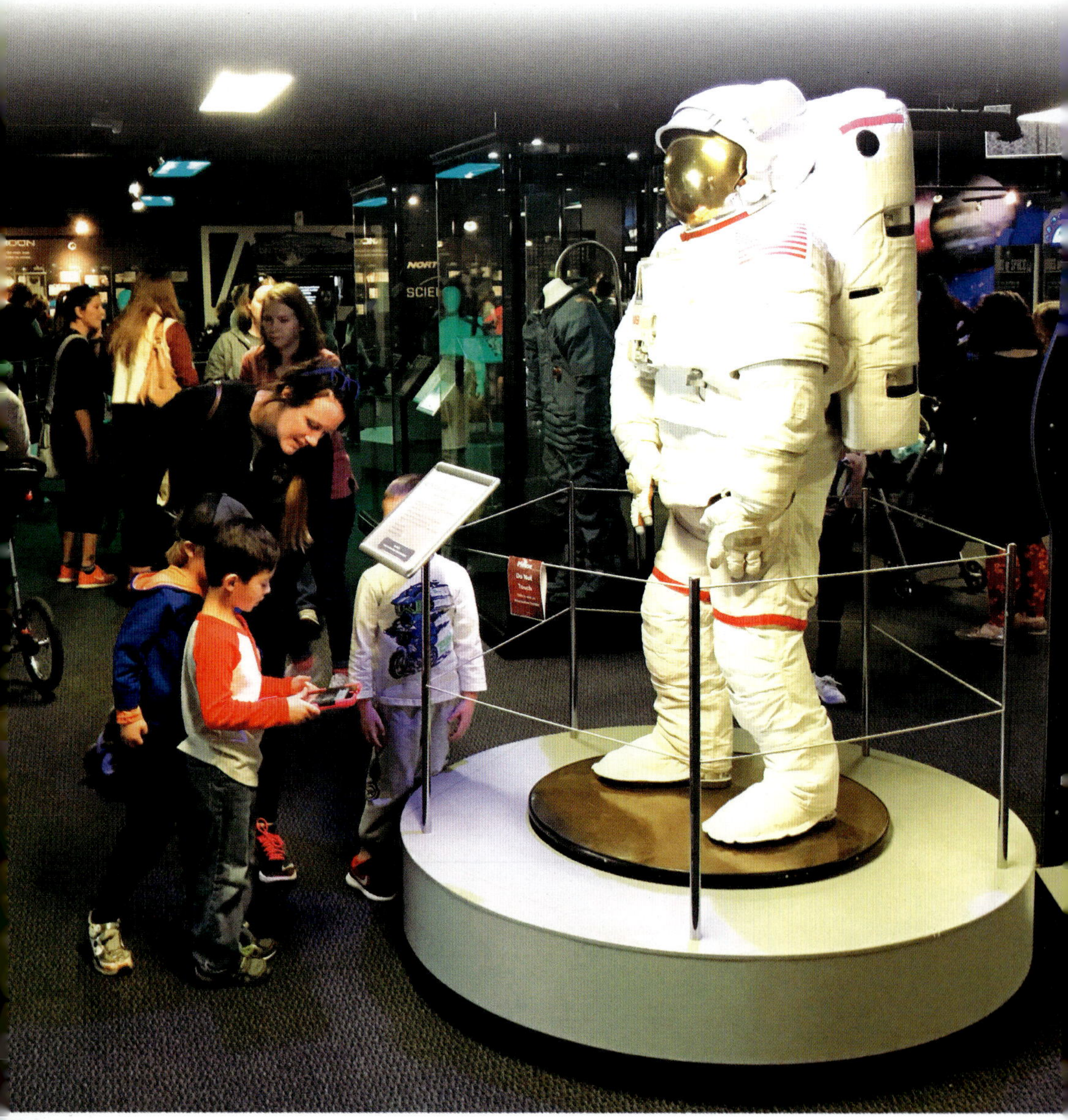

El Pomar Space Gallery

Exhibits a wide variety of space artifacts.

Lockheed Martin Space Education Center

Offers hands-on activities and demonstrations with state-of-the-art STEM equipment.

Northrop Grumman Science Center

Displays the universe through a dynamic spherical projection system that brings the Earth, Sun, Moon and other planets to life.

FAMILY FUN

Rocky Mountain Dinosaur Resource Center

Dinosaurs in the Rockies? Really? Yes, right here in Woodland Park! Just a scenic 30-minute drive from Colorado Springs is one of the most comprehensive dinosaur centers in the world. More than 60 life-size prehistoric specimens are on display, including the 'bambiraptor', one of the most complete raptor skeletons ever found in North America.

Visitors can peek inside the Paleontology Lab to watch the scientists and paleontology technicians at work.

The Children's Learning Center offers hands-on learning and many activities for busy minds. Here, the kids can brush off fossils in the dig box, read books, create their own dinosaur or watch a fun and informative movie.

GOOD *to Know*

Guided tours are **included** in the admission

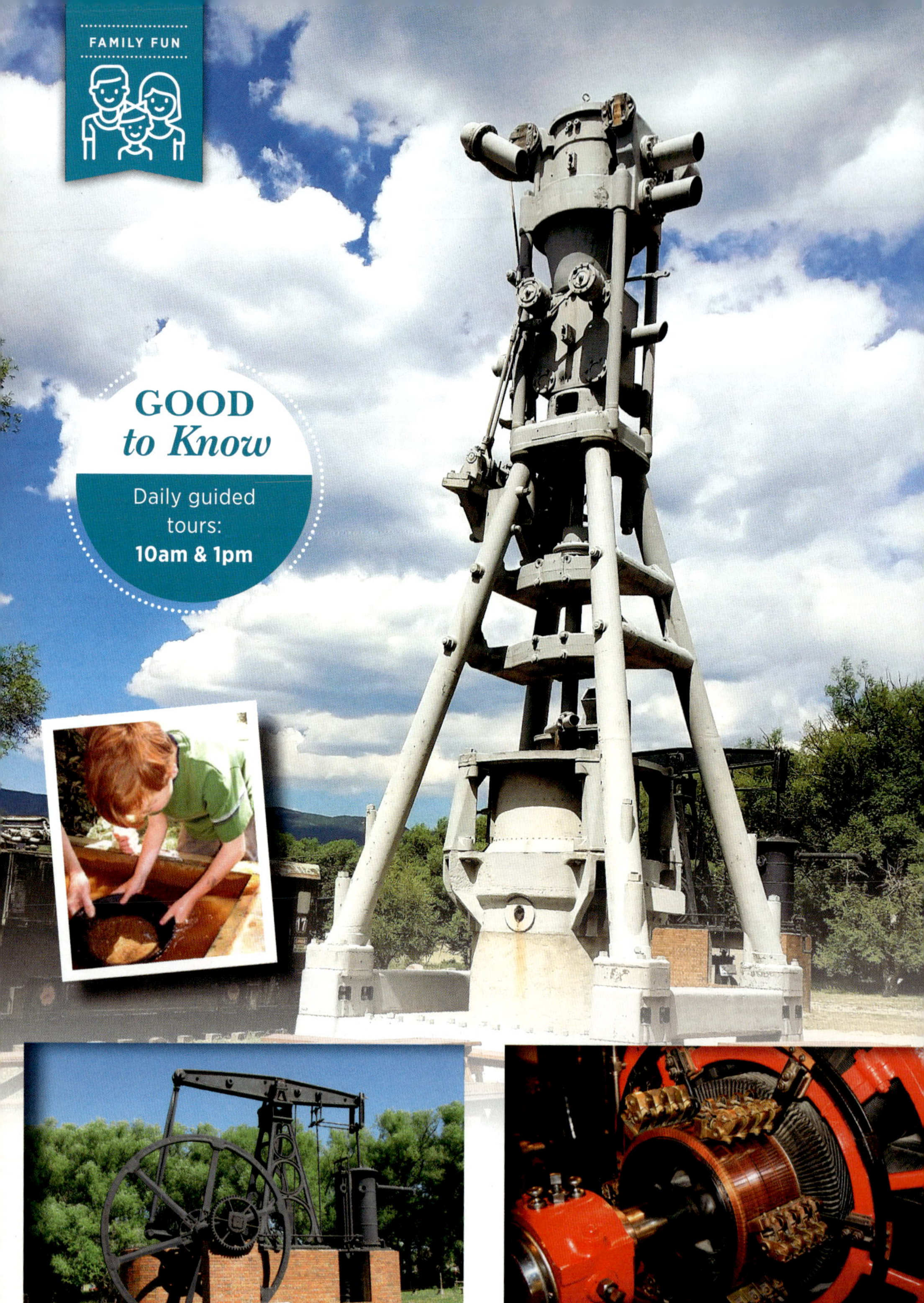
FAMILY FUN
GOOD
to Know
Daily guided
tours:
10am & 1pm

Western Museum of Mining and Industry

Talk about a hands-on experience for the entire family! The Western Museum of Mining and Industry is a 27-acre indoor/outdoor venue that is guaranteed to surprise you and put a lot of fun in a family day. From dynamic guided tours to interactive exhibits and educational events, this museum offers something for everyone! Want to experience what life was like in the 1890s? Dress up like a miner and learn to gold pan like a pioneer! Or learn about what "rocks" you eat and witness a 37-ton steam engine in operation ... this is the place that has it all.

Pikes Peak Marathon

Fruitcake Toss

Territory Days

Emma Crawford Coffin Races

Annual Events

There is hardly a weekend without a festival in the area. Here are just a few of the unique events not to be missed...

Fruitcake Toss - January

The fruitcakes will fly once again in downtown Manitou Springs!

Territory Days - May

Step back in time and watch performances by Native American dancers, Wild West gunfight re-enactments and live blacksmith demonstrations.

Held each Memorial Day weekend in Old Colorado City.

Pikes Peak or Bust Rodeo - July

Saddle up for five days of cowboy fun at the Norris-Penrose Event Center.

Pikes Peak Marathon - August

Racing 13 miles up to the summit of Pikes Peak and back, this may just be the most elevating marathon in the world.

Emma Crawford Coffin Races - October

In 1891 Emma Crawford, who loved the charming town of Manitou died of tuberculosis. Her wish to be buried on top of Red Mountain was fulfilled. In 1912, it is said her coffin was washed down the mountain. In her honor, each October, the Emma Crawford Coffin Races and Parade celebrates this unusual story.

Please check out **VisitCOS.com** for a more complete list.

Pikes Peak or Bust Rodeo

Emma Crawford Coffin Races

43
FUN FACT!
On the Friday before the race is **Fan Fest** the area's largest street festival!

Pikes Peak International Hill Climb

The race is on ... each year, in late June, the thrilling Pikes Peak International Hill Climb, aka "Race to the Clouds", is held in the area.

The first hill climb took place in 1916, making this tradition the second oldest motorsport event in America!

In 16 different classes of vehicles, about 130 competitors risk it all when they race the 12.4-mile course up to the 14,115-foot summit. The speed will amaze you: the current record is just under 8.14 minutes!

Colorado Springs Labor Day Lift Off

Each Labor Day weekend, one of the largest hot air ballooning events in the country is happening right here. For three beautiful September days, Colorado Springs transforms into a colorful air balloon mecca during this annual tradition.

More than 60 hot air balloons converge in Memorial Park for a picturesque display of color and fire. This festival offers something for the whole family - live entertainment, chainsaw carving, donut eating and balloon photo contest, concerts, skydiving and lake activities. There is also a beer garden and plenty of food trucks.

GOOD *to Know*

Free admission

Royal Gorge

The Royal Gorge, a scenic 45-minute drive south, is an amazing canyon cut by the raging waters of the Arkansas River. It is a canyon of superlatives ... at 1,250 feet deep, it is one of the deepest canyons in Colorado and, being only 50 feet wide in places, also makes it one of the narrowest.

Since the opening of the Royal Gorge Bridge and Park in 1929, the Royal Gorge has become a popular tourist destination. Walk across the bridge to enjoy the breathtaking views or go for an exhilarating zip-line or aerial gondola ride across the canyon.

FUN FACT!

The bridge held the title of the **"world's highest"** from 1929 until 2001.

NEARBY

Want to experience "the trip that bankrupts the English language" like President Teddy Roosevelt did in 1905? Climb aboard the Royal Gorge Route Railroad and delight in a scenic train ride along the Arkansas River through the majestic Royal Gorge canyon while enjoying a delicious breakfast, lunch or dinner, even a murder mystery.

GOOD *to Know*

Seating is limited. Make your reservations early.

Royal Gorge Route Railroad

This journey is sure to leave you with unforgettable memories of the Rocky Mountains. Welcome aboard!

Arkansas River Valley

Barely an hour's drive from Colorado Springs, the wild but gorgeous Arkansas River winds its way through stunning canyons and valleys. With more than 152 rafting miles and more than 80 Class II to Class V rapids, the Arkansas River is undoubtedly the nation's most popular whitewater rafting destination.

FUN FACT!

There are more than 120 "eries": wineries, breweries, eateries, galleries, roasteries, and distilleries in the Arkansas River Valley.

Between Leadville and Canyon City alone, the Arkansas River offers 80 miles of public access and superb trout-fishing conditions. Numerous campgrounds are scattered along the Arkansas River, surrounded by the majestic beauty of many of Colorado's 14,000 ft. mountains. There is no shortage of activities all throughout the Arkansas River Valley: rafting and kayaking, hiking and biking, horseback-riding, four-wheeling and zip lining ... or just relax and take in the awe-inspiring ambiance.

NEARBY

Located about an hour north is Colorado's largest city and state capital, Denver.

Founded in 1858 along the South Platte River and the Front Range of the Rocky Mountains, Denver quickly grew into a bustling metropolis with a population of about 2.8 million people.

FUN FACT!

Denver, the Mile High City, lies **5,280 feet** above sea level.

Denver

The breathtaking views of the snowcapped peaks of the Rocky Mountains and a multitude of attractions, festivals and sights, make Denver a great daytrip destination.

Red Rocks Amphitheatre

Ski Towns

Only a short 2-hour drive from Colorado Springs lie some of the best ski resorts in the Rockies. Scenic Interstate highway 24 snakes west from Colorado Springs into the High Country.

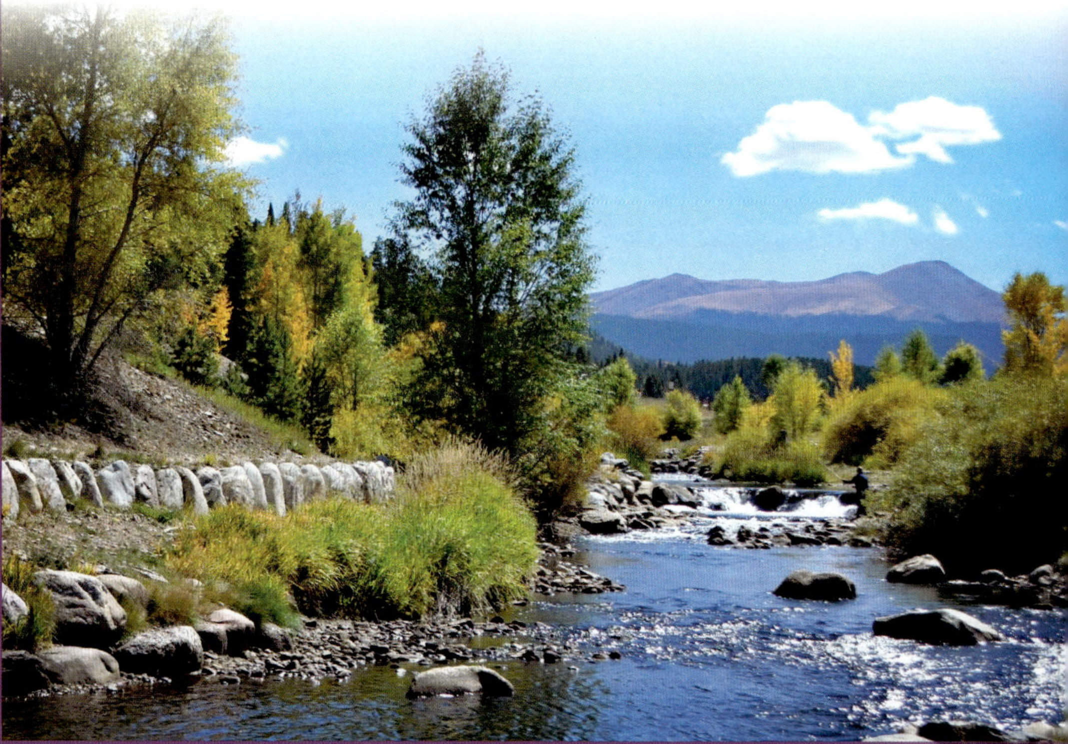

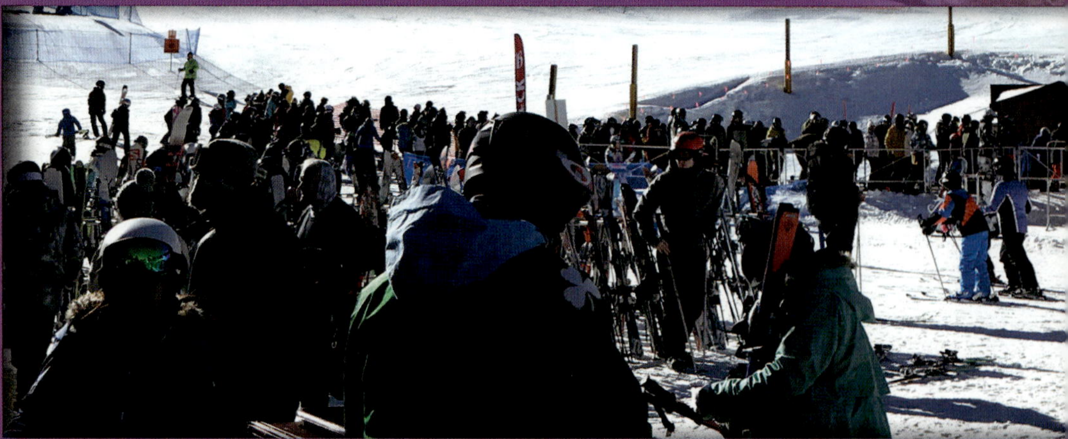

Winding through amazing rock formations and quaint old mountain towns, suddenly the landscape opens up to a vast mountain meadow overlooking the majestic Sawatch Range. The Sawatch Range is a magnificent mountain range with eight of the twenty tallest peaks in the Rocky Mountains, including the highest, Mount Elbert.

FUN FACT!

The 6 ski areas offer about **17,000** skiable acres!

Summit County is part of the High Rockies, or High Country, and greets you with a surplus of vividly charming mountain towns, like Breckenridge, Frisco, Silverthorne, Keystone and Copper Mountain. An abundance of outdoors activities for the whole family surrounded by the awe-inspiring natural beauty of this part of the Rockies makes this area perfect for both, summer and winter getaways.

Breckenridge, Keystone, Copper Mountain and Arapaho Basin are also major ski resorts offering a bountiful variety of ski terrain, fit for everyone.

The pristinely beautiful town of Vail and it's neighboring resort of Beaver Creek, are just a quick drive away and add even more possibilities for outdoors fun – in the snow and the sun!

NEARBY

Eleven Mile Reservoir

Picturesque Eleven Mile State Park can be reached within an hour's drive from Colorado Springs. The 7,662-acre park envelopes a 3,405-acre lake. It is one of Colorado's largest reservoirs known for it's excellent trout fishing conditions and thriving Kokanee salmon population.

With lots of amenities, including a marina, a visitor's center, over 300 campsites, gorgeous trails, playgrounds and picnic areas, this park offers an array of activities like fishing and boating, hiking and biking, all while wrapped in the majestic beauty of the Rockies.

As with all state parks, a park entry vehicle pass is required and can be easily purchased at the entrance to the park. The cost is $7.

Keep in MIND

The reservoir is known to be **very windy** in the afternoon.

Cripple Creek

The historic town of Cripple Creek, roughly an hour to the west, sits at an elevation of 9,494 feet on the southwest slope of Pikes Peak. Cripple Creek and its neighboring town, Victor, are famously intertwined with the Gold Rush era.

After the Gold Rush, the towns transformed from lively mining towns to forgotten ghost towns. Today's visitors can choose from a variety of experiences such as descending into a historic gold mine, riding a steam locomotive or simply trying to "strike gold" in one of the many casinos.

DON'T *Miss*

The annual Ice Festival in February.

Did you KNOW?

The fossils are estimated to be **34 million years old**.

Florissant Fossil Beds

Underneath a grassy mountain valley sprawls one of the most opulent and diverse fossil deposits in the world! About 1,800 fossil species of insects, birds and plants – even 14 foot wide petrified Sequoia trees – are on display.

The Florissant Fossil Beds National Monument is just off Interstate 24, 40 miles west of Colorado Springs.

Hiking and Biking

Within minutes of downtown Colorado Springs, there is an amazing array of parks, open spaces and trails to satisfy the souls of hikers and bikers of every level ... and even dog lovers! Here are some of the most popular:

Garden of the Gods / Easy

Paved and gravel trails wind through incredible red rock formations with stunning views of Pikes Peak.

Red Rock Canyon Open Space / Easy to Moderate

This gorgeous canyon offers a variety of trails along lakes and stunning rock formations and even an off-leash dog area.

Cheyenne Mountain State Park / Easy to Moderate

Located just south of Colorado Springs, this splendid 2,700-acre park offers 20 miles of trails.

Palmer Park / Easy to Moderate

A 737-acre wildlife preserve located on a mesa overlooking the city and mountains.

Bear Creek Dog Park / Easy

Just west of downtown, this 25-acre off-leash park is an exciting place for leisure walks with your favorite canine.

Barr Trail / Difficult

This infamous 12-mile trail takes you from the town of Manitou Springs to the summit of Pikes Peak at 14,115 ft. Not for the faint of heart, this trail gains 7,800 feet.

Austin Bluffs Open Space / Easy to Moderate

With nearly 500 acres of unique rock formations this park offers everything from paved trails to difficult single tracks for riders and hikers of all levels.

North Cheyenne Cañon Park / Easy to Moderate

Enjoy a scenic drive on the old Gold Camp train bed and you'll find dozens of scenic overlooks and trailheads. Some mentionable hikes include Helen Hunt Falls (Silver Cascade) and Seven Bridges.

Fishing Colorado Springs

Whether you prefer a rambling stream or a picturesque lake, wearing waders or floating in a boat, you will find an amazing variety of beautiful fishing locations in the Pikes Peak region.

Here are just a few notable angler destinations:

North Slope Recreation Area

On your way up toward Pikes Peak you will find the Crystal Creek Reservoir.

Arkansas River

About an hour south, this fast flowing river offers challenges for all levels of fly fishing enthusiasts.

Fountain Creek

Located in Manitou Springs, this creek is a great place to take the young ones for a morning of fishing.

Monument Lake

Not to be confused with Monument Lake Resort in Southern Colorado, this serene lake is located just north of Colorado Springs.

GREAT OUTDOORS

Family Activities

The Pikes Peak region is a mecca of fun for all ages! From rock climbing and rafting to zip lining and horseback riding, there is absolutely no shortage of activities. Please check out **VisitCOS.com** for even more exciting deals and ideas.

Golf Courses

Colorado Springs' unique location with Pikes Peak as a stunning backdrop and mild, sunny weather offers near year-round golfing - with unmatched views.

Here are a few of the golf courses to enjoy:

Valley Hi Municipal Golf Course
Patty Jewett Golf Course
Garden of the gods/Kissing Camels Golf Course and Resort
Pine Creek Golf Club
Country Club of Colorado
Colorado Springs Country Club
Silver Spruce Golf Course
World Golf and Sand Creek Golf Club
Cherokee Ridge Golf Course
Spring Ranch Golf Club

Prefer Disc Golf:

Cottonwood Creek Disc Golf Course
Rampart Disc Golf Course
Aviary Disc Golf Course
Sand Creek Disc Golf Course

Symbols of Colorado

State Flag

State Bird: Lark Bunting

State Fish: Greenback Cutthroat Trout

State Insect: Colorado Hairstreak Butterfly

State Mammal: Rocky Mountain Bighorn Sheep

State Reptile: Western Painted Turtle

State Flower: Rocky Mountain Columbine

State Cactus: Claret Cup Cactus

Wildlife of Colorado Springs

Big Horn Sheep

Coyote

Mule Deer

Mountain Lion

Fox

Mountain Goat

Bobcat

Bears

Elk

Index